How to Perform Your Five Daily Prayers

STEP BY STEP GUIDE

BEGINNER FRIENDLY

ACCORDING TO THE QURAN AND SUNNAH

ANESA VUCETOVIC FERATOVIC

Islam consists of Five Pillars, which are made obligatory for each Muslim to fulfill. These Five Pillars are as follows:

1) The Testimony of Faith (Shahada):
"La ilaha illa Allah, Muhammadur rasoolu Allah." This means "There is no true god (deity) but God (Allah), and Muhammad is the Messenger (Prophet) of God."

2) Prayer (Five Times a Day)

3) Giving Zakat (Charity for the Needy):
The word zakat refers to purification as well as growth. Giving zakat means giving a specified percentage on certain properties that one owns to specific classes of needy people.

4) Fasting the Month of Ramadan

5) Pilgrimage to Makkah

Before praying you must take Wudu (purification).

Allah says, "Surely Allah loves those who turn to Him and those who care for cleanliness." (2:222)

There are a few things that can invalidate your prayer and your Wudu:

1) Any trace of human urine
2) Any trace of bodily fluids (male/female)
3) Menstrual blood

In certain situations you are required to only take Wudu prior to prayer and in other situations you are required to take Ghusl.

When to take Wudu:
If any of these occur: natural discharges such as urine and/or excrement, passing gas, and falling asleep (deep sleep where you are not aware of whether or not you broke your wudu).

When to take Ghusl:
This includes washing the whole body from head to toe, which can happen if one experiences unconscious ejaculation (in their sleep), post-childbirth bleeding, menstruation, or intercourse.

"O you who believe! When you intend to offer As-Salaah (the prayer), wash your faces and your hands (forearms) up to the elbows, rub (by passing wet hands over) your heads, and (wash) your feet up to the ankles. If you are in a state of Janaaba (i.e. after a sexual discharge), purify yourselves (bathe your whole body). But if you are ill or on a journey, or any of you comes after answering the call of nature, or you have been in contact with women (i.e. sexual intercourse), and you find no water, then perform Tayammum with clean earth and rub therewith your faces and hands. Allaah does not want to place you in difficulty, but He wants to purify you, and to complete His Favour to you that you may be thankful" [al-Maa'idah 5:6]

WUDU (Ablution):

One must perform Wudu in order to purify themselves prior to prayer so that their prayer may be accepted.

1) Make your Intention:
Say Bismillah (In the name of Allah) in your heart and that the purpose of you taking Wudu is to fulfill Allah's obligation and prepare yourself for Salah.

2) Wash both your right and your left hands up to the wrists beginning with your right hand three times each. While doing so, be sure that the water has reached between the fingers.

3) Take water while using your right hand, put it into your mouth and rinse well three times.

4) Take water while using your right hand, slightly inhaling it into your nose and blow it out three times. (Use the left hand to help blow it out).

5) Repeatedly wash your entire face three times. (That which includes: between the right ear to the left ear, and your forehead all the way to the bottom of your chin).

6) Take water in your right palm and wash your right arm all the way to your elbow three times. Be certain that no part of your arm is left unwashed. Do the same with your left arm.

7) Take water in both your palms, enough to slightly wet over your head starting from the top of your forehead to the back of your head (all the way down to where your hairline ends before your neck). Then bring both hands over back to the forehead.

8) Then put your index fingers in your ears and wipe the back of the ears with your thumbs.

9) Lastly, wash both feet to the ankles three times, beginning with your right foot. Be certain that the water has reached between the toes and no spot has been left dry on the foot.

Once you have finished taking Wudu, recite (outside of the restroom):

"Ashhadu alla ilaha illallahu, wa ash-hadu anna muhammadan abduhu wa rasuluhu."

Which means:

"I bear witness that there is no deity worthy of worship except Allah alone, and I bear witness that Muhammad is His servant and His messenger."

If you put clean socks on after you took Wudu and you happen to nullify it, then you are able to wipe over your clean socks once when you retake it following the same steps. This applies for only one day and one night if you are not traveling and for three days and nights if you are traveling.

If for some reason you do not have any water and can't perform Wudu in time before the next prayer, there is another option for you. It is considered Wudu using the earth as a resource. It is called Tayammum. The way tayammum is done is by saying Bismillaah with the intention of performing Tayammum. You then go over the ground once with the palms of the hands, then wipe the back of your right hand with the palm of the left, and the back of your left hand with the palm of the right. And lastly, you wipe the face with both hands. You then are to recite the same dua that is recited after wudu, after you completed Tayammum.

After performing Tayammum a person is pure and may perform prayer.

"All of the earth has been made for me and my nation a pure place of prayer. Whenever a person from my nation wants to pray, he has something with which to purify himself, that is, the earth." (Related by Ahmad)

Call to Prayer (Adhan)

When making the call for prayer, stand facing the Qiblah and raise your hands to your ears and call out:

Everything that has been narrated in the Sunnah about the adhaan is considered permissible. It is recommended that one should recite one version sometimes and another version sometimes, so that it will not cause confusion and fitnah (tribulation).

.Allaahu akbar, Allaah akbar, Allaahu akbar, Allaah akbar, ash-hadu an laa ilaah ill-Allaah, ash-hadu an laa ilaah ill-Allaah, ash-hadu anna Muhammadan rasool-Allaah, ash-hadu anna Muhammadan rasool-Allaah. Then he should repeat, ash-hadu an laa ilaah ill-Allaah, ash-hadu an laa ilaah ill-Allaah, ash-hadu anna Muhammadan rasool-Allaah, ash-hadu anna Muhammadan rasool-Allaah. Hayya 'ala al-salaah – twice; hayya 'ala'l-falaah – twice; Allaahu akbar, Allaahu akbar, Laa ilaaha ill-Allaah

Iqaamah (right before the fard prayer, if praying in congregation)

Several forms of the iqaamah have been narrated from the Prophet (peace and blessings of Allah be upon him).

The first form::
Allaahu akbar, Allaah akbar; ash-hadu an laa ilaah ill-Allaah; ash-hadu anna Muhammadan rasool-Allaah; hayya 'ala al-salaah, hayya 'ala'l-falaah; qad qaamat il-salaah, qad qaamat il-salaahAllaahu akbar, Allaahu akbar; Laa ilaaha ill-Allaah

The Messenger of Allah (peace and blessings of Allah be upon him) said: "Dua is not rejected between the adhan and iqamah, so engage in dua (supplication)."

There is a specific dua to be narrated immediately after the adhan:

It was narrated from Jabir ibn 'Abd-Allah (may Allah be pleased with him) that the Messenger of Allah (peace and blessings of Allah be upon him) said:

Whoever says when he hears the call to prayer:

Allahumma Rabba hadhihi'l-da'wat il-tammah wa'l-salat il-qaimah, ati Muhammadan il waseelata wa'l-fadeelah, wab'athhu maqaman mahmoodan illadhi wa'adtah

O Allah, Lord of this perfect call and the prayer to be offered, grant Muhammad the privilege (of intercession) and also the eminence, and resurrect him to the praised position that You have promised), my intercession for him will be permitted on the Day of Resurrection.

Shortening Prayers

The meaning of shortening prayers is that the four rakat prayers become two rakats when traveling. Shortening the prayers is considered better for the traveler than performing them in full, because the Prophet (peace and blessings of Allah be upon him) shortened prayers during all of his journeys.

As for joining prayers, it means that the believer joins two prayers, Duhr and Asr, or Maghrib and Isha, at the time of the earlier or later of the two prayers. Joining prayers is permissible for every traveler, as well as for the person who is not traveling only if it is too difficult for him or her to offer every prayer on time.

WUDU: Visual Representation

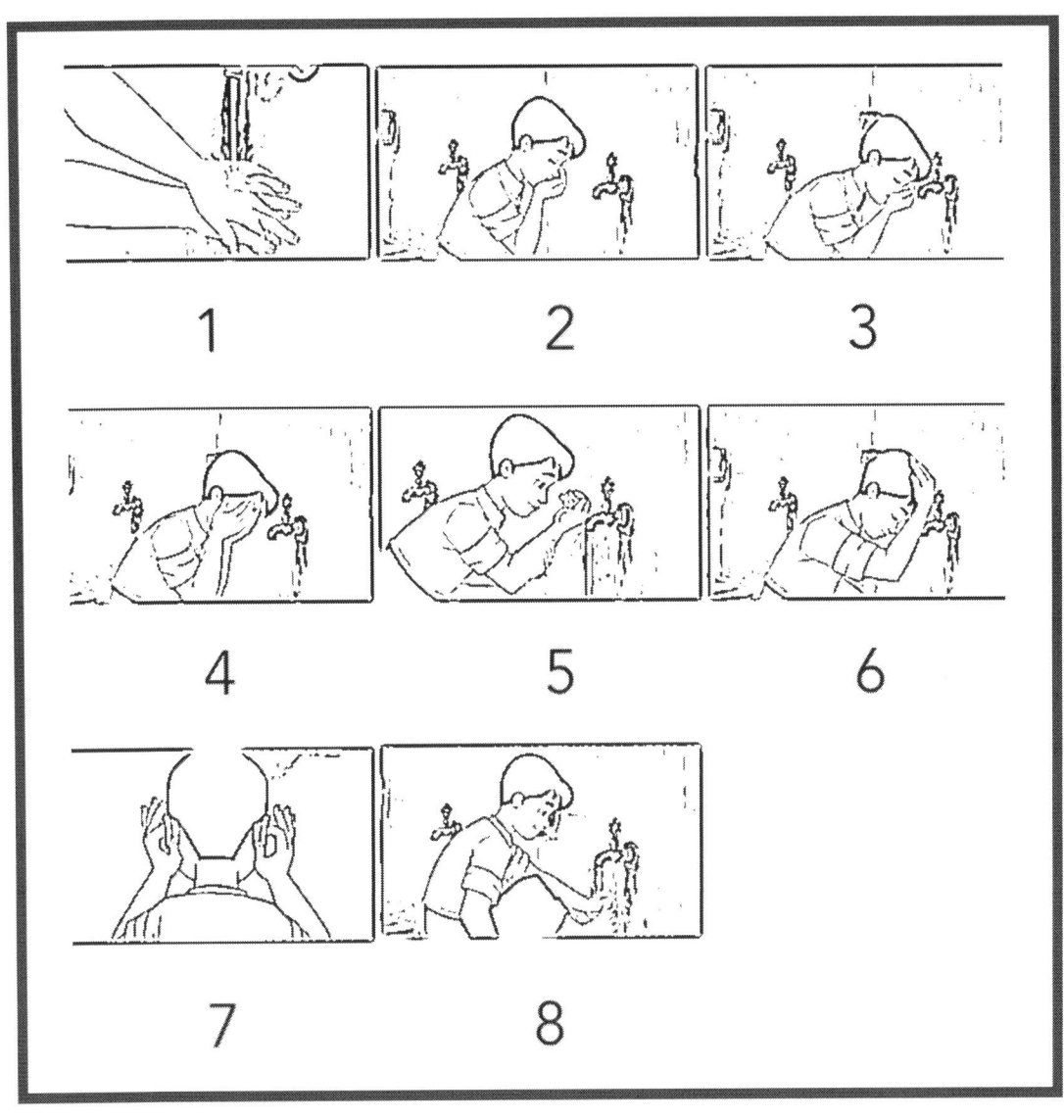

The Prophet (Blessings and peace be upon him) said: "The line of demarcation between a Muslim and a Kafir is the giving up of Salah." (Sahih Muslim)

Which means, the prayer is like a barrier between Kufr (disbeliever) and Islam, so whoever does not pray, he will enter in Kufr (he will be a disbeliever).

Prayer Chart
(Prayer times depend on your location)

PRAYER	Sunnah (before Fard)	Fard	Sunnah	Witr
Fajr	2	2		
Dhur	2+2	4	2	
Asr	4	4		
Maghrib		3	2	
Isha	4	4	2	1 or 3 (odd number rakat)

A Muslim is required to pray five times a day. The mandatory prayers are called Fard prayers in Arabic.

Make sure you have Wudu and be sure that you are wearing clean clothing that are appropriate for prayer. For males, clothing that covers from the navel to just below your knees and a shirt that covers ones shoulders. For females, clothing that isn't tight and covers every part of your body (other than your face and hands) including your feet (socks may be worn).

How To Perform Salah (Prayer)

1) Stand in an upright position with your body facing the direction of Al-Ka'bah. This position is known as Qiyaam and the direction is known as Qiblah in Arabic. The Qiblah varies from location; in North America it is towards the east with a slight angle towards the North.

2) Make your intention (*Niyyah*) in your heart for the prayer you plan on performing.

3) Raise both hands to your ears and say "*Allah Akbar*" which translates to *Allah is the Greatest.*

4) Next, place your right hand on top of your left hand on the chest and look downward to the place where your forehead and nose will touch the ground in Sujood (prostration) and recite:

"*Subhanaka allahumma wa bi hamdika wa tabara kasmuka wa ta'ala jadduka wa la ilaha ghairuka.*"

This translates to: "O Allah, how perfect You are and praise be to You. Blessed is Your name, and exalted is Your majesty. There is no god but You." [This supplication, Subhanaka, is only recited once at the beginning of the first Rakat.]

5) Then recite Surah Fatiha,

Audhu billahi-minash-Shaytanir-rajeem.
Bismilla-hir-Rahmaanir-Raheem.
Alhamdu lillahi Rabbil-'alameen.
Ar-Rahmanir-Raheem. Maliki yawmid-deen. Iyyaka na'budu wa iyyaka nasta'een. Ihdinassiratal-mustaqeem. Siratal-ladheena an'amta 'alayhim, ghayrilmaghdoobi 'alayhim walad-dalleen. Ameen (Surah Fatiha 1:1-7)

Translation:
I seek refuge with Allah from the accursed devil (Shaitan).
In the Name of Allah, the Most Gracious, the Most Merciful. All praise and thanks are Allah's, the Lord of the 'Alamin. The Most Gracious, the Most Merciful. The Only Owner of the Day of Recompense. You (Alone) we worship, and You (Alone) we ask for help. Guide us to the Straight Way. The way of those on whom You have bestowed Your Grace, not (the way) of those who earned Your Anger, nor of those who went astray.
(Surah Fatiha 1:1-7)
Note: Always recite Surah Fatiha in every rakat. If this Surah is not recited then your Salah will be invalid.

6) Next, recite any other passage from the Noble Qur'an. (Always during the 1st and 2nd rakat after Al-Fatiha)
An example would be: Surah Ikhlas

"*Bismilla-hir-Rahmaanir Raheem.*
Qul huwal-lahu ahad.
Allahus-Samad.
Lam yalid wa lam yuulad.
Wa lam yakul-lahu kufuwan ahad.

Translation:
In the Name of Allah, the Most Gracious, the Most Merciful. Say: Allah is Unique! Allah is the source [for everything]; He has not fathered anyone nor was He fathered, and there is nothing comparable to Him!
(Surah Ikhlas 112:1-4)

7) Then say: "*Allahu Akbar*" picking your hands up by your ears again and then bowing down placing your hands on your knees and silently saying: "*Subhana Rabbiyal Adhim.*" This means: (How Perfect is my Lord, the Supreme) three times. This position is referred to as Ruku. Keep your head in line with your back (90 degree angle), and look downward to the place of Sujood.

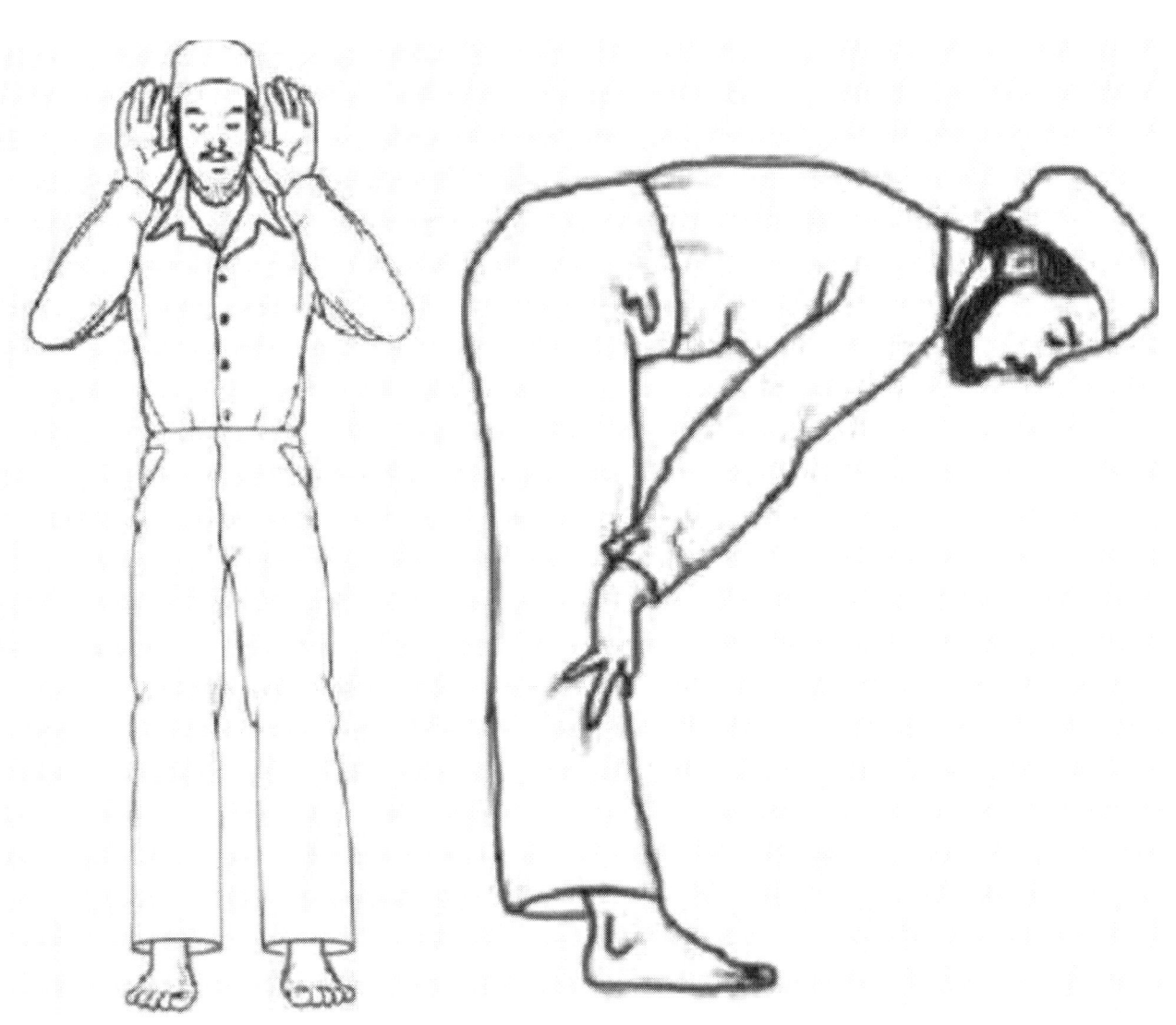

8) Then you are to stand up straight from the bowing position saying: *"Sami Allahu liman hamidah"* Translates to: (Allah hears those who praise Him)

And then before you prostrate say, *"Rabbana lakal hamd."* Translates to: (Our Lord, praise be to You).

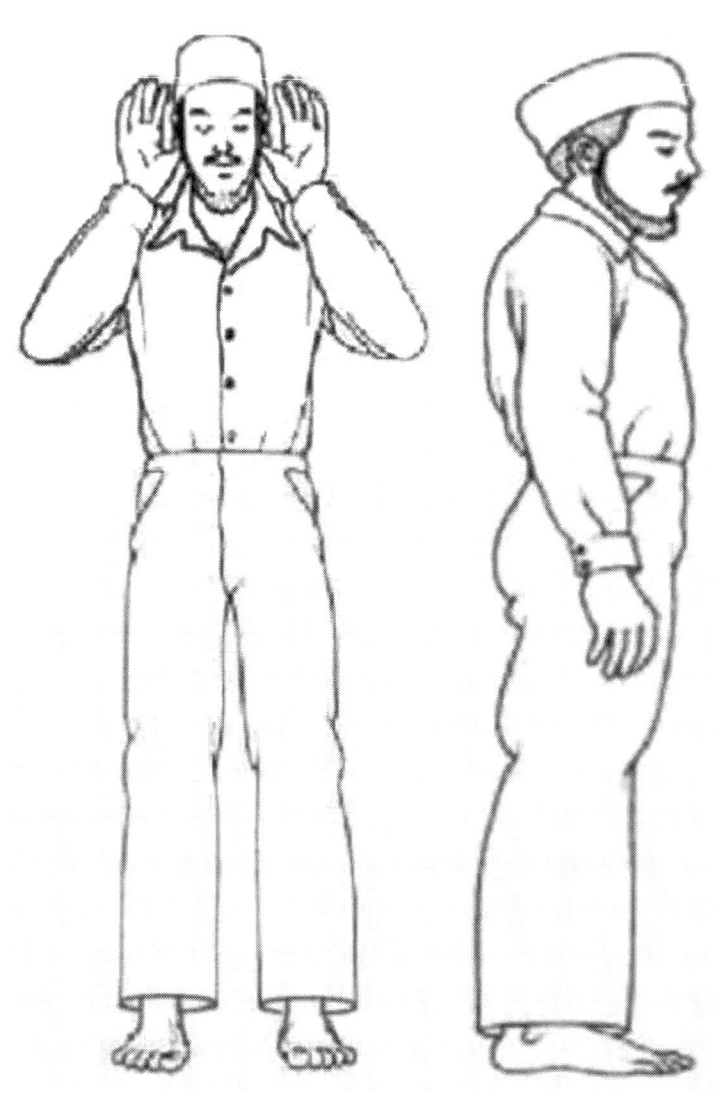

9) While going to the floor in prostration say "*Allahu Akbar*" with your forehead, your nose, and both your palms, your knees, and your toes touching the floor. Then you are to recite, "*Subhana Rabbiyal A'la*" Translates to: (How Perfect is my Lord, the Highest) three times. This position is known as Sujood; be sure to keep your arms away from touching the sides of your body and the ground.

10) Then sit up from the prostrating position saying "*Allahu Akbar*". Make sure you are sitting upright with your knees bent and both your palms placed on them and say: "*Rabbighfir li.*" Translates to: "O my Lord! Forgive me."

Say "*Allahu Akbar*" and go down in prostration again in Sujood and recite "*Subhana Rabbiyal A'la*" three times. Then sit up from this position while reciting "*Allahu Akbar*" one time.

Make sure your right foot is this way.

Up until this point you have completed the first Rakat or unit of Salah. Now you are to stand up for the second Rakat and repeat the same procedure reciting all parts except you do not recite Subhanaka at the beginning. Subhanaka is only recited at the start of the very first Rakat. After the second Sujood (prostration) you sit on your left leg while keeping your right foot upright and you place both hands on your thighs. The right hand on your thigh with all fingers together in a fist except for your index finger. Stick the index finger straight out (in a pointing position). Put your left hand flat on the left thigh.

11) Now you are to recite *Tashahhud* silently:

At-tahiyatu lillahi was-salawatu wat-tayyibatu assalamu ʿalayka, ayyuhan-nabiyyu wa rahmatullahi wa barakatuhu, as-salamu ʿalayna wa ʿala ʿibadul-lahissaliheen. Ashhadu alla ilaha illallahu wa ashhadu anna Muhammadan abduhu wa Rasuluhu.

All the compliments, prayers and good things are due to Allah. Peace be upon you, O Prophet and Allah's Mercy and Blessing be on you. Peace be on us and on the true pious devotees of Allah. I testify that none has the right to be worshipped but Allah and I testify that Muhammad is His slave and His Messenger.

Then recite silently *Assalatul-Ibrahimiyah*:

Allahumma salli 'ala Muhammad wa 'ala ali Muhammad kama sallayta 'ala Ibrahim wa 'ala ali Ibrahim innaka HameedumMajeed. Allahumma barik 'ala Muhammad wa 'ala ali Muhammad kama barakta 'ala Ibrahim wa 'ala ali Ibrahim innaka Hameedum-Majeed.

O Allah bestow Your favor on Muhammad and on the family of Muhammad as You have bestowed Your favor on Ibrahim and on the family of Ibrahim, You are Praiseworthy, Most Glorious. O Allah, bless Muhammad and the family of Muhammad as You have blessed Ibrahim and the family of Ibrahim, You are Praiseworthy, Most Glorious. (Sahih Bukhari)

Lastly, you are to recite:

Allaahumma 'innee 'a'oozu bika min l'azaabil-qabri, wa min 'azaabi jahannama, wa min fitnatil-mahyaa walmamaati, wa min sharri fitnatil-maseehid-dajjaal.

O Allah, I seek refuge in You from the punishment of the grave, and from the punishment of Hell-fire, and from the trials of life and death, and from the evil of the trial of the False Messiah. (Bukhari and Muslim)

12) Now you are to turn your face first to the right while saying *"Assalamu alaikum wa rahmatullah"* (may peace and mercy of Allah be on you) and then turn to the left repeating those same words.

You have completed the Two Rakat Salah.

As we stated, some prayers have more than two Rakats. Dhur (4), Asr (4), and Maghrib (3). The entire procedure is repeated except after Tashahhud during the second rakat prostration, you are to say Allahu Akbar and stand up only reciting Al-Fatiha in the 3rd and 4th rakat while standing and following each step we mentioned for the Two Rakat Salah (Ruku, rising, Sujood/Prostration).

In the last rakat of any prayer, after you made your Sujood and you are sitting upright be sure to recite Tashahhud and Salatul Ibrahimiyyah. At the end of any prayer, you must finish by giving salaam (Salutation); turning your head from right to left and repeating:

As-salaamu 'alaykum wa rahmatullah
Peace be upon you and the Mercy of Allah.

The Two Rakat Salah

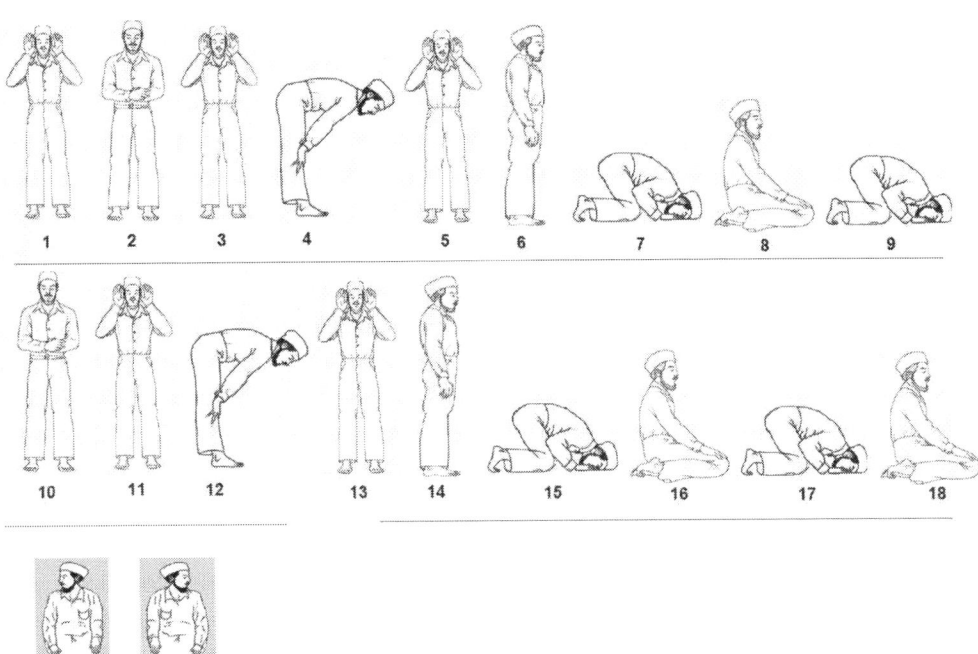

Witr Prayer:

Allah has prescribed for you a prayer (by which He may increase your reward), which is Witr; Allah has enjoined it for you during the time between 'Isha prayer until dawn begins."

The With prayer is an odd number of rakats prayed after Isha prayer and before Sunrise. During the Witr prayer, recite Surah Al-Fatihah and another Surah from the Qur'an. Before or after Ruku' of the last Rakat raise both your hands high to the level of your shoulders and recite the following Dua with your hands raised towards the sky.

This Dua is called Dua al-Qunut:

Allahumma Ihdeni Fiman Hadayt, Wa A'feni Fiman A'fayt, Watawallani Fiman Tawallayt, Wabarek li Fima A'atayt, Waqeni Sharra Ma Qadayt, Fainaka Taqdi Wala Yuqda 'Alayk, Wainnahu La Yadhilu Man Walayt, Tabarakta Rabbana Wat'alayt.

Translates to:
O Allah, guide me among those whom You have guided. Grant me safety among those whom You have granted safety. Take me into Your charge among those whom You have taken into Your charge. Bless me in what You have given me. Protect me from the evil that You have decreed, for You decree and nothing is decreed for You. And there is no humiliation for whom You take as a ward. Blessed and exalted are You, our Lord.

Once you have completed this, say: "*Allahu Akbar*" and bow down in Ruku and complete the rest of your prayer following the same steps mentioned for the rest of your prayer.

Things that invalidate your prayer:

1) All things mentioned previously that nullify Wudu.
2) Laughing
3) Talking
4) Dressing inappropriately
5) Drinking or eating
6) Not facing the Qiblah

If you miss a prayer:

You are required to make it up. Make sure to pray your prayers in chronological order even if you missed it. For example, if you missed Dhur, and it is now Asr, then you must make the intention of performing Dhur first and then Asr.

Things that are permissible during prayer:

1) To pray with shoes on, if the shoes are not considered impure
2) If you must carry a baby
3) Take a few steps while making sure your shoulders are facing Qiblah if it is needed

After you give Salaam (after Fard prayers):

The Prophet (peace and blessings be upon him) used to recite:

Subhan'Allah 33 times
Alhamdulillah 33 times
Allahu Akbar 34 times

The Prophet (blessings and peace be upon him) once said to his Companions: "If there was a river at the door of anyone of you and he took a bath in it five times a day, would you notice any dirt on him?" They said, "Not a trace of dirt would be left." The Prophet (Blessings and peace be upon him) said: "That is the example of the five obligatory prayers with which Allah blots out evil deeds." (Sahih Bukhari and Sahih Muslim)

"Verily, the prayer keeps one from the great sins and evil deeds" (Surah al-Ankaboot)

"The first matter that the slave will be brought to account for on the Day of Judgment is the prayer. If it is sound, then the rest of his deeds will be sound. And if it is bad, then the rest of his deeds will be bad." (Recorded by al-Tabarani)

Allahu Alam.
Allah knows best.